# The Language of Stone

Poems

# The Language of Stone

Poems

Joan Dobbie

First U.S. edition 2019

Editor and Publisher:   Laura LeHew

Proofreaders:            Nancy Carol Moody
                         Keli Osborn

Cover Art:               "untitled photograph" © Joan Dobbie


Copyright © 2019    Joan Dobbie

Uttered Chaos
PO Box 50638
Eugene, OR 97405
www.utteredchaos.org

All Rights Reserved. Except for brief passages quoted in a newspaper, magazine, radio or television review, no portion of this book may be reproduced in any form or by any means, electronic or mechanical, including photocopying and recording, or by any information storage and retrieval system, without written permission from the Publisher. All rights to the works printed herein remain with the author.

ISBN: 978-0-9998334-6-9

In memory of Noelle Vial who said, "Stone. Slash. Isolation. Now write."

With thanks to Cecelia Hagen, Michael James, Jean Murphy, Elaine Weiss and Ken Zimmerman, who were kind enough to read and comment when these poems first came into being. Special thanks to Erik Muller who, two decades later, helped mold this manuscript into a viable book and to Erica Goss whose enthusiasm and videography allowed some of these poems to cross the line between print and screen.

With a huge grateful thank you to *The Language of Stone*'s publisher Laura LeHew of Uttered Chaos.

## for Michael

### STONES DO NOT MOVE

They don't move.
They just sit there
forever in rows.

Under them boxes.
Boxes of bones.
Dirty old bones.

Sprinkle my ashes over the ocean.
Sprinkle my ashes into the wind.
Teach me to fly. Let me fly.

# CONTENTS

| | |
|---|---|
| THE PEACH'S ROUGH STONE | 1 |
| IN CHILDHOOD | 2 |
| THE MAN IN THE HAMMOCK | 3 |
| THE SEA AND THE DESERT | 4 |
| THE OLD MAN WHO LOVED STONES | 5 |
| THE WORLD | 6 |
| THERE WAS AN OLD WOMAN | 7 |
| THE DEVIL | 8 |
| IT FELL FROM THE SKY | 9 |
| THE STONE THAT WAS SHAPED LIKE A BOY | 10 |
| HOW THE STONE DIFFERS FROM THE HUMAN | 12 |
| STONE AMONG BUTTERFLIES | 13 |
| THE STONE THAT WAS SHAPED LIKE A GIRL | 14 |
| A MAN FELL IN LOVE | 15 |
| THE VISIT | 16 |
| THAT KIND OF STONE | 17 |
| THE STONE AND THE OLD WOMAN | 18 |
| LOVE SONG IN THE LANGUAGE OF STONE | 20 |
| TWO STONES OR ONE STONE | 21 |
| STONES DO SING | 22 |
| THE STONE THAT FELL INTO THE SEA | 23 |
| THE STONE TURNED TO A SPONGE | 24 |
| A LITTLE PINK TONGUE | 25 |
| HOW TO HAVE SEX WITH A STONE | 26 |
| TWO PEBBLES | 27 |
| THE WOMAN WHO TURNED TO STONE | 28 |

| | |
|---|---|
| THE VOICE THAT IS OLDER THAN STARS | 30 |
| THE RIVER STONE | 32 |
| THE DAUGHTER | 33 |
| WHAT IT'S LIKE LIVING INSIDE OF A STONE | 34 |
| THUS SPAKE THE RAIN | 35 |
| LAWN DECORATION | 36 |
| SORROW | 37 |
| INNER SUBURBIA | 38 |
| THE WOMAN WAS GOING | 39 |
| THE OLD WOMAN AND THE SEA STONE | 40 |
| TWO LONELY STONES | 41 |
| THE TERRIBLY DIFFICULT STONE | 42 |
| TEN MINUTES TO CLOSING | 43 |
| OBSESSIVE STONE | 44 |
| THE BOULDER IN THE LIVING ROOM | 45 |
| PANNING FOR GOLD | 46 |
| WINDOWSILL GODS | 47 |
| THE BUCKET | 48 |
| THE HUNGRY STONE | 49 |
| JUST BEFORE SUNSET | 50 |
| NIGHT AFTER NIGHT | 51 |
| WHY THE MOUNTAIN WAS SO POWERFUL | 52 |
| SHE STOOD THERE UNTHINKING | 53 |
| HOW TO CLEAN STONES FROM YOUR CARPET | 54 |
| AS I WAS WALKING | 55 |
| HOW TO GET OUT FROM UNDER A STONE | 56 |

| | |
|---|---|
| DREAM CITIES ARE MADE OUT OF STONE | 57 |
| THE LOST STONE | 58 |
| LIBERTY DINER | 59 |
| BIRTH OF A MEADOW | 60 |
| THE GODDESS SHE CARVED OUT OF STONE | 61 |
| THE WOMAN WHO LEARNED TO LOOK DOWN | 62 |
| STONES DO NOT FLOAT | 64 |
| NOTES | 67 |
| ABOUT THE AUTHOR | 69 |
| ACKNOWLEDGMENTS | 71 |

## THE PEACH'S ROUGH STONE

The peach's rough stone
holds a life in its belly.
The dove's egg is a soft stone
filled with promise of bird.

The future of marble
depends on the sculptor.
The pipes of an organ
are molded from lead.

What then can be said
of the stone that is human?
How much heat can it bear?
How much weight
      without cracking?

Is there somewhere within it
a dark viscous fluid
that properly tempered
might learn how to sing?

Is there bone
      in the angel's wing?

# IN CHILDHOOD

In childhood I carried a stone
in my stomach.
Later it rose to my heart,
now it's stuck in my throat.

Sometimes I wake to it
hot between my legs. Sometimes
it's cold in my chest, or drilling
a hole in the pit of my stomach.

Sometimes I take it in my hand,
hold it to my cheek, pop it
like a lozenge into my mouth,
rolling and rolling

it over my tongue. Once in the
demon-filled night
I threw it up over my head
high and hard. I was young then.

I could throw overhand.
It soared
like a fast ball, clearing
the trees of my childhood, rose

till it struck solid sky, where
it stuck—till I swallowed it.

# THE MAN IN THE HAMMOCK

If you are a child, for
example, of three
maybe four, and you
and your sister drop
two children's
handfuls of clattering pebbles
over the ridge of a hot
Brooklyn rooftop
those stones either do
or do not
strike the sound
asleep head of
that man in the hammock
seven stories
below and you run
away laughing
and grow up
never knowing.

## THE SEA AND THE DESERT

The sea stone and the desert stone met
at the shoreline.

Early one morning just after sunrise
when the world was still pink
with beginning.

Sandpipers lifted their tiny forked feet
tickling one, then the other,
and all of the sand in between.

*Once*, spoke the sea stone, *seawater
caressed me over and under
until I succumbed into pleasure.*

The desert stone nodded. *Just so
was the wind once my lover.*

*A tortoise swam by*, sighed the sea stone,
*stroking my back with its needle-fine claws.*

*Just so*, smiled the desert stone. *Once
in the high heat of summer, a tortoise
crept under my belly for shade.*

*Bones*, said the sea stone, under the swell
of the wave, *they grow smooth.*

*Bones, ah yes, bones*, the desert stone
sighed, as the sea began lapping
her body.

## THE OLD MAN WHO LOVED STONES

There was an old man
who loved stones, those that were
shapely, the ones he could hold onto for
lifetimes in his hand
without dropping, though once
he did drop one.

For ten thousand years
he searched for his stone.
He searched through
the marshes and watery places,
searched in the dark
halls of libraries, searched

in the steeples of
skyscrapers, searched in the temples,
in the cellars of churches, searched
through the ruins
where forests had grown.

He searched in the deserts,
in the mountains, searched
till he finally
came to the sea,
and kept searching.

He searched till his feet
melted off underneath him
and still he kept searching…
searched till his skin became scaly
with fins and his hair

became pale as the foam
on the sea. He searched till
he finally found his lost stone
and he never let go.

## THE WORLD

God made the World
out of stone.

Goddess shrieked:
*How could you do this
to me?*

*I made it first.
I made it of water.*

## THERE WAS AN OLD WOMAN

There was an old woman
who walked in the desert.

Everything there
in the dry sand was dead.
Even the flowers

that once had held water
now were just crusts

where once water had been.
And walking one day

through that graveyard
of flowers
stubbing her toe

she discovered a stone—
such an odd, heavy stone.

## THE DEVIL

The Devil decided:
*Today, I will be a stone.*

So he walked on this earth
in the guise of a stone

and she who chanced to pass
him on the road

was moved to turn
and kneel beside him

and lay her hand
upon him.

## IT FELL FROM THE SKY

Moon woman—what could she do?
When that stone fell at her feet
she'd picked it up

without thinking,
let it lie in her pocket
round as a small moon.

For eons it lay there,
innocent as a lost bird
but so terribly hungry.

And as it waxed
so she waned,
the sky painting her black.

Its voice swallowed her voice.
Its name swallowed her name.
And the years turned to dust in her hand.

## THE STONE THAT WAS SHAPED LIKE A BOY

Its head was too big.
It got stuck in its mother.

The doctor had to use his knife
to cut it out.

The mother used her fist
to keep it in shape.

Its heart shriveled up.
Its heart was as small

as a raisin.

In its youth it killed spiders
and ants.

It even killed ladybugs.

It blushed and it cried
for its mother.

The cruel boys laughed at it.
They said that it acted

like a girl.

The girls stayed away from it.
They called it *the baby*.

The *frou-frou*.

It was afraid to grow up,
afraid of man's sadness.

Once it had seen a grown man
it called father.

crushing a stone
with his huge heavy tool.

It was afraid of the man's
roar and stench.

It wanted to hide in the sea
of its mother.

But its mother had died long ago,
herself eaten by time

and all that was left to call mother

was parched as the desert
in August.

It was a sad, lonely stone, and oh,
how it thirsted for the sea.

## HOW THE STONE DIFFERS FROM THE HUMAN

Unlike the human
the stone
has no nerves

on its skin

which may feel as smooth
as live flesh
to the touch

but itself

cannot feel
anything
except its own weight—

the pressure of time.

The stone that is carved
to the shape of a man
can even be kissed

but itself cannot kiss.

Can be
taken to bed
and used as a dildo

but cannot make love.

## STONE AMONG BUTTERFLIES

It was the only
stone in the world, the only
one anywhere, ever to be.
All around it as far as
the eye could see
grew hedgerow and clover,
milkweed, dandelion, mustard
and foxglove. Sometimes the sun
warmed it, the rain
cooled it. Blankets of
snow covered it
for months at a time. Once
a loquacious flock of butterflies
lit on its surface, all of them speaking
at once: some spoke in the language
of just waking up, some in the
language of falling asleep. Some giggled
in accents of go-find-your-sweetie or whispered
the rose-budding dialect. Nearly all of them
fluent in wind through the meadow grass, but
none of them, none, spoke
the language of stone.

## THE STONE THAT WAS SHAPED LIKE A GIRL

Everyone
thought it was real. It had

soulful round eyes and small fingers.
It smiled for the camera.

When it was dressed in a
pretty white dress

it recited a poem.
When it was given a small

silver fork
it ate up its dinner.

When it was given a boyfriend

it opened its legs and
when it was given a husband

it washed up the dishes.
But when it was left

by itself

at the edge of the highway
then it did

nothing. After all, it was
only a stone.

## A MAN FELL IN LOVE

A man fell in love with a
cool, white stone
that was

smooth as marble
and as impenetrable—
though it was not marble.

He kept
the stone near him
wherever he went:

teased it, caressed it,
in all ways
made love to it.

And though
the stone neither warmed
nor opened

his life was less lonely,
more holy,
because of it.

## THE VISIT

That woman, she was
so terribly lonely
that when the stone

knocked at her door
she invited him in.

*Forever, I think,*
said the woman,
*I have been waiting.*

*Well, I have come,*
said the stone.
*Now open your heart.*

*But you smell like a stone,*
said the woman.
*My heart will not open.*

Then he got out his chisel
and worked on her heart.

But that heart
was hard as a rock
and so it remained.

## THAT KIND OF STONE

It's that kind of stone
that fits like a plum, like a
breast in your hand, fits

like a skull in your hand, like
sexual organs when they are swollen
with blood.

That kind of stone.
Whenever I touch it
I hate it.

Whenever I'm not touching it
my hands tingle and ache
for the feel of it.

If I could I would
throw it away. If I did
I would spend the rest of my life

sifting sand through
my fingers, creeping through
dirt

on my belly, molding
mud into shape with my fingers.

## THE STONE AND THE OLD WOMAN

Said the stone
to the old woman, *Love me,
I need love.*

*All right,*
said the woman, *I'll try.*

And she carried him
into her bed. He was cold
and hard, so she got out her
knife and chiseled away

at him. She chiseled
two arms and two legs.
The arms were to hold her.
The legs were for dancing.

They were cold and hard
and stiff, but they sort of worked.

*What's wrong, woman?
Why don't you love me yet?*

*I'm trying,* she answered.
And she chiseled a face
with blue eyes and a cute
little nose. Then she started

the beard. *No beard*
snapped the stone
with his shiny new tongue.
*I want to look young.
Why don't you love me enough?*

*You won't have a small beard?
NO!*

And then when she kissed
his new lips
they were cold and hard.
And his round cherry cheeks.
And his fists.

## LOVE SONG IN THE LANGUAGE OF STONE

There once was a man
who carried a stone
in his pocket.

Sometimes he pulled out
his stone and threw it

at some woman's face.
He didn't really mean to,
he just couldn't help it.

The stone had a life of its own.

Sometimes the woman
whose face was all bruised

sat down and cried because
something was hurting so badly.

It wasn't really her fault,
she didn't mean to.
Her tears had a life of their own.

One time the sun shone on her tears
making them sparkle like diamonds.

One time the rain fell on his stone
making it shine like a jewel.

That man and that woman, I think,
somehow loved one another.

Those tears, that stone
were the words to a love song,
the song that the mourning dove sings.

## TWO STONES OR ONE STONE

Two broken stones went bumpily
bouncing side-by-side

down a steep jagged mountain.

*God, this is fun!* sighed the one.
*God, how this hurts*, cried the other.

Both stones were brittle and hard.
Bouncing, they struck one another.

*Oh, don't let this end*, cried the one.
*Oh, please let it end*, sighed the other.

After many long years
they came to a valley.

By then they were round stones
and lay in soft silence

side-by-side in the grass
by the highway.

A car drove by fast. Then another,
then another.

Do you think someone finally stopped
to go walking?

Do you think someone picked up a stone
for his hand, a stone

for his pocket?

Do you think someone picked up a stone
for her altar? A pretty round stone?

Two stones or one stone?

## STONES DO SING

It happens sometimes
when they strike

one another
under

the fast-spinning
rush of a creek

that has just woken
up for the spring.

## THE STONE THAT FELL INTO THE SEA

A stone sank in the sea far and deep,
the sea that was hungry.

Saltwater swallowed him, water so heavy
the stone could not breathe.

For ten thousand years he
lived in the sea without breathing.

He grew a tough shell like the sea snail,
feelers and ink like the squid:

suction-cupped fingers that swept
through the dark wavy waters

endlessly searching.
One day an old woman swam in the sea.

The stone grabbed her ankle and pulled
with his long inky tentacles.

He sucked her up into his shell
moaning, *Love me, I need love.*

*If you keep me I'll die!* cried the woman.
*Only a stone can live without breathing.*

But the hungry sea swallowed her voice
and the stone was deaf anyway.

## THE STONE TURNED TO A SPONGE

The stone turned to a sponge
and leapt
on the woman.

It opened its
ten thousand mouths

and devoured her.

## A LITTLE PINK TONGUE

The stone
had a little pink tongue.

It could draw in its tongue
making it moist
push it back out

and then wiggle the tongue
like a little pink worm.

Inside the stone
were ten thousand tongues
all sizes and colors

some of them strong
as an elephant's trunk.

But only the little pink tongue
had a window to peek through.

If anyone bent close enough
to try kissing the stone

it would stick out
its little pink tongue.

## HOW TO HAVE SEX WITH A STONE

First you must love it, must learn
to be in love with it. Study its
form and its shape, run your hand
over it nightly. Capture its image.
Keep it in your brain.
Then you must open your mouth
wide as you can, stick out your tongue
(moisten it first) and acquire
a taste for the stone.
Not any stone, this stone.
Smell is important.
Some stones smell earthy. Those
are quite easy to love. Others
due to their years underground
carry within them the lost smell
of death. Worms crawl about them.
Those you must coddle.
Forgive them their funereal odor,
their inconsolate darkness.
*Stone swallow death*,
you must whisper in their ear,
*and grow green with it.*

## TWO PEBBLES

Two pebbles lay side by side
at the edge of the highway.

Said one to the other,
*Hold me, I need love.*

    *How can I? I have no arms.*

*Sing to me then.*

    *I have no voice.*

*All right then,*
*just lie here beside me.*

    *Yes, but the night is long.*

## THE WOMAN WHO TURNED TO STONE

There was an old woman
who met a young stone
that was shaped like a snake
with a jewel on its forehead.

The jewel was a sharp
diamond crystal.

*Now you must love me*
hissed the snake at the woman
rocking his crystal
in front of her eyes.

And the moon rose.
And the moon set.
And the moon rose.

The old woman stared as he
glided his cold reptilian fingers
over her warm human body
in dry scaly ripples.

And her salty lips spread
in a smile as he sang in her ears
with his slender
        split tongue

while his jewel flashed
in the moonlight.

And then when he kissed her
a long icy chill
swept through her body
like wind through the desert.

*I love you*, she lied
in a dry scaly whisper
as she felt herself turning

to stone.

## THE VOICE THAT IS OLDER THAN STARS

She lived in a world that was made
out of stone. Though she was a flesh
and blood woman, and inside her flesh
and blood heart lived a voice. It was
a lonely voice, a voice full of longing.

*Somewhere*, the voice crooned
the refrain of her childhood,
*my man waits for me.*
But this was a lie. For her man was not
whole. A demon named
time had cut him up into pieces.

Part of him lived in the east, part of him
lived further east. Part of him lived
at the source of the world. Only the part
that was made out of stone
remembered her name.

One day a stone man knocked at her door.
He looked like a whole man, but he was
only the part that was made
out of stone. *I am the dream
of your childhood* he told her. *I cost only
two souls.*

*No thank you* she answered. *I just
can't afford it.*

But he was a large stone, and bold. He broke
through her doorway, rolled over her
threshold, flattened her rug. *Just
let me love you* he whispered. *That's
all I ask.* And his breath was so cold
that it turned her to stone. Even her flesh
and blood heart turned to stone.

The man stone and the woman stone
bumped at each other, making loud rhythmic
crashing for many long years.

While inside her stone heart
an old fire kept burning. Inside that fire
an icy voice screaming.

## THE RIVER STONE

A stone lay in the riverbed.
Water ran over her day after day,
night after night—cool water with fishes.
But the stone was not happy.

*Someday*, said the stone, in a
soft dreamy whisper,
*someone will walk in the water.*

*Someone will pick me*
*up in his hand, carry me*
*home in his pocket. And then*
*I'll be happy.*

And it happened that someone
did walk in the water, picked her
up in his hand, carried her home

for his bookshelf—
where she lay alone year after
year, under layers of dust
untouched and forgotten.

And the stone dreamed of her riverbed.
And in dream she was happy.

## THE DAUGHTER

A stone woman gave birth
to a daughter of stone.

The two stones
looked exactly alike

but they rolled
down the mountain

on opposite sides.
*I am here* called the mother,

sending her voice as a snake
over the mountain

in search of her daughter
holding tight to its tail.

*I am gone* called the daughter
knocking the snake on its head

with the diamond sharp
fist of her

short broken childhood.

## WHAT IT'S LIKE LIVING INSIDE OF A STONE

It's dirty of course, dark
stuffy, cold. No cushions
to sit on, just the rough floor.
Just some ashes.
No windows. No doors.
You vaguely remember
how you got in there
but you're not really certain
and anyway that opening
closed years ago. Just forget
about that one. Stop pounding
your fists
at the wall, stop
staring at nothing. Sit yourself
down for a while. I know
it's a drag, just sit down anyway.
Sit facing the wall, and take
some deep breaths. Breathe in
and breathe out. Do you see
that white light—tiny white light—
in the distance? Inhale that white light
till it fills the vast space
of you.

Now open your wings.

## THUS SPAKE THE RAIN

The stone did not melt in the rain
nor did it soften. Moss did not grow

on its surface and the shape of the stone
did not change. The rain

fell in droves, fell for years,
fell forever. Lilacs and daffodils

sprouted in the rain, budded, bloomed,
faded and withered, never

once tasting sunshine. Rainwater
covered the stone day and night

wailing: *Come with me... come with me...*
but the stone did not budge.

*This stone is a master of patience,*
thus spake the rain.

## LAWN DECORATION

There are those who put
stones in their lawns

rather than grass
or gardens or shrubs:

Stones are quite easy—
no need to water
          or trim them.

Nothing to harvest.

Even the grasshoppers shun them.

Stones are quite beautiful,
lying inert in soft shadowed silence.

They hardly remember the sea.

# SORROW

A stone stood
at the mouth of the river.

It was a sentinel stone.
Its head was the shape of

a library lion, teeth glistening
ivory, fangs long & curved

like the fangs of a
saber-toothed tiger.

Whenever a lie
tried to enter the river

the stone tore it open
spilling its entrails into the water

that bled like a
sea of lost babies

filling the basin
with sorrow.

## INNER SUBURBIA

### 1.

A stone fell on the woman.
It crushed her
into a thousand small pieces

that lay flat as gravel, dead
as a driveway in summer.

Under the weight of that stone
nothing could move anymore. Nothing
could grow.

### 2.

A car
parked in the driveway,
sun charring the steering wheel, seat
almost melted. Burnt window,
cracked frame.

No one
to get in the car, no one
to drive the hell out of there.

### 3.

No one at home in the house, the house
that was empty. No one to answer
the phone, no one to open

the fridge or to care
for the dog, the dog
that was howling.

## THE WOMAN WAS GOING

insane.

Her brains were all

scattered.

Inside her head

was the rattle

of pebbles.

If there was a gem

in there anywhere

she couldn't

find it.

# THE OLD WOMAN AND THE SEA STONE

There was an old woman
who carried a stone

in her hand.
It was a sea stone.

It had lived all its life
underwater.

*Would you like to be young?*
said the stone.

*Yes*, sighed the woman.
*Oh yes.*

With a clamshell he scraped off
her wrinkles.

*Now you are young*, said the stone.
*Do you want to be beautiful?*

*Yes, yes, oh yes.*

He let the seawater polish her face
for ten thousand years.

*Now you are beautiful*, said the stone.
*Do you want to be loved?*

*How?* said the woman.

*I don't know*, said the stone
as it slipped from her hand

sinking away in the sea.

## TWO LONELY STONES

lay side by side
in the riverbed.

Water flowed over them
making a sound

almost holy.

Sand slipped away
underneath them
so fast

it seemed like the earth
was falling away
moment by moment.

*Perhaps we should dance,*
whispered one to the other.

*Do you think we should dance?*
whispered the other to the one.

But they were just stones
and stones have no ears.

Neither the one
nor the other could hear

so they just lay there unmoving
year after year.

## THE TERRIBLY DIFFICULT STONE

It was beautiful, yes, but heavy
as sin, and expensive.

They are always expensive.
Nor did she have the right tools,

and no matter
how hard she worked far

into the wee hours
chipping away at it, still

it was never quite right. It just
kept getting smaller, and somehow

less beautiful…
This stone she was feeding

her life to, it was far
less than human. It was

not even art. It had never
been alive.

## TEN MINUTES TO CLOSING

The couple is frozen in stone, and so
they'll remain until the stone crumbles.
Signs read: *Please Do Not Touch.*
A video camera stops you from running

your sensitive fingers over the breasts of the woman,
the thighs of the man, as you so long to do.
If you dared you would take out your chisel,
crack open the woman's white chest and enter

her body. Once inside that body, you wouldn't
leave it sit frozen in sweet modest nakedness
kissing forever that stone white stone man.
You'd dress it in wild satin lace, black as manure,

raise up the bull from his strawberry meadow
and fuck till the cows came home singing.

## OBSESSIVE STONE

I'm talking about the kind of stone
that requires another
kind of stone
for power

Like a magnet
Like iron

I'm talking electricity
I'm talking desperation

I'm talking about
a kind of madness
that rises like a

mountain
        crazed &
                spitting fire

over everything
that ever lived

## THE BOULDER IN THE LIVING ROOM

That monstrous stone was too heavy to move.
It was un-moveable.

If you wanted to enter the house
you had to squeeze in around the edges of it

and make yourself thin as a rail
scraping your entire body between its dark

raspy surface and the rough plaster wall.
Sometimes your skin would start bleeding.

You had to put up with the bleeding.
If you wanted to leave the house

you had to climb over the entire bulk of it
and once you got to the door you had to

find some way to pry the door open
and squeeze yourself out.

You were drained as an old rag
long before you ever hit the street

and once you were out on the street
you didn't want to ever come home.

You wanted to travel the world,
       sing
              shout
                       swallow the sky.

But you had to come home.
The stone needed feeding.

## PANNING FOR GOLD

There is gold in the brook
by your feet, both
granite and gold.

Scoop the sand up in your cup
swish back and forth
like the sea.

Little stones fall by the way
but the gold, heavy gold
stays behind

and no matter how much
you have found
there is never enough.

## WINDOWSILL GODS

The man stone and the woman stone
hold hands forever

on her windowsill
over the sink.

Whenever she washes the dishes
she prays to the stones.

Whenever she fixes a meal
she pours milk on the stones.

She is waiting for the man stone
to actually move, to leap

to his feet and get the hell
out.

She is waiting for the woman stone
to gracefully rise to her feet, to

raise up her arms in a blessing and finally
open her mouth.

## THE BUCKET

was filled up with stones.

If you tried to pour water
into the bucket, it gurgled out
over the top, making a waterfall

first, then sinking away
turning the earth black.

If you tried
to pick up the bucket and move it
you couldn't. Its thin wire handle

would cut through your hand
drawing blood, but the bucket
itself wouldn't budge.

If you tried to kick over the bucket
it was like kicking over a brick wall
with your bare foot.

There was an old woman.
She kicked at the bucket
for ten thousand years.

## THE HUNGRY STONE

It was a radiant stone,
a dangerous stone—a stone
women died for. It caused

old ones to tremble and snap
at the root, their faces
to crack like the earth

during drought. It caused
young ones to smile till their faces
burst open, drowning in sweetness.

Women were fruit
and the stone ever starving.
*Peel yourself open for me*

the stone whispered,
its voice rich with hunger
as it swallowed them whole.

## JUST BEFORE SUNSET

The man and the woman are holding
each other down

underground.

Once they were soft
as moist clay,

each with the sensitive
hand of a sculptor

molding the other.

Now they are brittle
as bone. Once they were nearly

transparent, each to the other
more light

than language, words almost
unnecessary. Now

they have nothing to say—

obtuse as two stones:
bookends in a library

of faults.

## NIGHT AFTER NIGHT

the stone
battled demons
tossing and burning.

Deep underground
the earth rumbled
in anger—

overhead, darkly,
a hurricane brewing.

## WHY THE MOUNTAIN WAS SO POWERFUL

For as long as the sky
could remember

a tiny gray pebble
lay quiet on the mountaintop

waiting for that
        golden eagle
                to swoop down

as in a dream
and carry her away

## SHE STOOD THERE UNTHINKING

at the edge of a cliff
gazing down into the
valley below.

Her one hand was still, resting
on the rough gnarled trunk
of a wind-twisted pine

that had managed somehow
to survive at this height.
In her other she held

a heavy round stone
smooth as a moon when
seen from the distance of earth.

A stranger walked by,
*Are you thinking to jump?*

The stone squirmed in her hand
as if it had life.

## HOW TO CLEAN STONES FROM YOUR CARPET

They are shit brown and hard
to see. Sometimes the eyes
refuse to focus
even on the large ones

even on those with jagged edges
that are dangerous, that can
cause your feet to bleed.

You must creep for long painful
hours on all fours
forcing your fingers
deep down to the root of each
individual strand.

When you feel something sharp
between your fingers
don't believe it's a jewel
—it isn't a jewel.

Yank it out now
with all your strength
like a tooth that's gone bad.
Throw it as far as you can
out the window, no matter

that it hurts like the devil. Life
always hurts, don't you know?

## AS I WAS WALKING

As I was walking
in the desert, every
tiny grain of sand
a tiny stone

I lay my body
like a baby, gentle
down upon my
bed of stones.

I let the sun burn
through my body,
let the blood flow
from my body

and the bitter
yellow sun
caressed my bones.

## HOW TO GET OUT FROM UNDER A STONE

If you find yourself deep
in the dirt

a dark stone
on your head

then you have to push up
with all of your strength.

Push against Gravity.
Push against Nature.
Push till the earth

splits apart all around you
and light enters in through the

top of your skull—
such brilliant light

you think you could scream
for the joy of it.

Push till your lungs
almost burst
with their hunger and

your lips open wide
in a wild toothy grin:

Push till it's over.
Push till you learn how to fly.

## DREAM CITIES ARE MADE OUT OF STONE

The streets are of stone,
the buildings of stone,
the ghats that lead down

to the water
are stone.

Even the water itself
is soft stone. The people,
the cattle, the ravens

are stone. The sun,
a hot stone, the sky,
a black stone, the moon

is no more than a stone
that is smiling
and the couple

that walks hand in hand
in the moonlight
gazes up into the moon's

smiling face, finding
heaven in stone.

# THE LOST STONE

A stone fell
from her hand. It was only

a small stone, not one
she had realized

was precious. But now
her hand ached for the

loss of it. She followed
the many long paths she had walked

holding the stone. Loosely
she'd held it, half hoping

(though never quite daring)
to drop it. Half wishing

she never had found it.
It had been such a rare stone, a cold

stone, burning like
ice in her hand

for so many years. Its coldness
had crept through her veins, sunk into

her bones. She had to admit she
almost had feared it. Where

had it come from? What
hazy sun had produced

such a stone? Why had it
fallen to earth? Why

had she found it only
to lose it?

## LIBERTY DINER

A salesman walked into
the Liberty Diner:

*Stones for Sale*
*Stones for Sale.*

Everyone was looking at the stones
slipping stones onto their fingers,
pressing stones against their throats, feasting
their vision on stones, touching stones.

Even the woman who
crouched in the corner, nursing starvation
reached for a stone.

*This is the stone of my childhood,*
she told them. *My birthstone, my
lifestone, my father's first gift.*

*This is the mirror
through which I escaped
when my dreams got too hungry.*

Setting it down, she walked
out the door.

The man selling mirrors
ran after the woman,

*STOP!* he cried,
placing the stone on her finger.

*Plant your dreams here
in the Liberty Diner.
Feed your dreams faithfully,
never betray them.*

## BIRTH OF A MEADOW

The girl was made wholly
of molten lava.
She poured herself

over the earth
and all of the flowers

died. There she lay
dreaming, black as
the highway.

There where she lay
was the end of the road.

All the trucks had to
slam on their brakes. Nothing
could move her, not even

time. Time only
cooled her. In time
she grew frigid,

all her dreams turned to stone.
And in time
the stone crumbled.

Tender green grasses
emerged then,
or so it is told.

## THE GODDESS SHE CARVED OUT OF STONE

There stood in the meadow a magnificent
boulder, grand as a monolith, alone
rising up from the meadow grass.
Rabbits built burrows beneath it,

hawks hovered over, and
butterflies perched on it.
The meadow itself
was hidden from human view.

Only one woman knew how to find it
and she never told anybody,
not even her children. But each time
she came to the meadow

she, with her hammer and chisel,
chipped one little chunk
from the monolith. This she would carry
away in her pocket, a gift for the

beggar in the street.
After many long years
there stood in the meadow
a goddess of stone.

Butterflies perched on her fingers,
hawks hovered over, and
snakes, green as meadow grass,
wove themselves into a tapestry
under her feet.

# THE WOMAN WHO LEARNED TO LOOK DOWN

One night while a girl slept
a demon crept into her room.
It cut out her heart and

put a round stone in its place.
When she woke the next morning
a gaping black mouth

was wailing in the space
between her breasts. That was
the day she started to bleed.

All the years after that
the mouth never stopped
wailing. The girl became woman,

the woman grew old. Her body dried up
like a leaf on the sidewalk. One day
she was walking in shadow

under trees. A jay on a low branch
called out her name. His voice
was a voice she almost
remembered.

*Joan*, he called, *just spit*. So
she spit the stone out of her chest
like a peach pit. Now her chest

was all empty. *I am hungry*,
the mouth in her chest
started wailing. *O I am hungry*.

And the jay laughed. He laughed
like a demon. Yet the berries that grew
by her feet were all shaped
like hearts. They were pink as the
bonnets of babies.

## STONES DO NOT FLOAT

They sink
right to the bottom, yet if

with the proper flip
to your wrist
                    you can
get them to skip
      on the top of the water

then they find themselves leaping
in moments of joy

and wherever they touch it
the water
       trembles

in an ever-widening arc
until it is everywhere touched.

## NOTES
A HISTORY OF STONES

In 1997, I think it was, the late Irish poet, Noelle Vial, came to Eugene, Oregon to lead a poetry writing workshop. My memory of it goes something like this: Noelle stood in front of a room of us and said, "Stone Slash Isolation (Stone/Isolation). Now write." And I did: one poem in her workshop and more and more and more from then on. They just kept filling my head and leaping out into my, back then, pretty new computer.

During this time, I was living with Michael James, now a dear friend, but then we were "in a relationship." And things were not going so well for either of us. Many of the stone poems, in the way that only poems can, seem to capture the individual, but also, universal, complexity of both his and my attempts to reach each other in ways that we couldn't... and my own inner need to break free. Others of the stone poems simply reflect my then stonish vision of pretty much everything in my life.

Michael, who was—and, in many ways, still is—an enthusiastic fan of my writing, insisted that I work on publishing this collection. He asked me to get advice, so I did, contacting friends in the poetry community: Cecelia Hagen, Jean Murphy, Elaine Weiss and Ken Zimmerman who were kind enough to give these poems thoughtful attention and useful feedback.

By now it was close to the millennium. Michael had moved to Manhattan, where he still lives, and I had moved to Boulder, Colorado, for what turned out to be a couple of years. A few of the poems found homes in various anthologies. I posted parts of the *Stone* manuscript on my website joandobbie.blogspot.com and sent it out, I think, once to a publisher I never heard back from. And... that was it. Except, as I tend to do with my poems, I enjoyed reciting one or another to myself now and then.

For years the stones sat underground deep inside my various computers, waiting for their time. Then, one evening in 2018, I think it was, at Laura LeHew and Roy Seitz' delightful *Poetry for the People* reading series, which included an open mic, I found myself sharing a few of them to what turned out to be a really enthusiastic audience. After the reading I went up to Erik Muller, asking if he'd be willing to advise me on the collection. His response, "I will only put energy into these poems if you agree to publish them." He suggested that Uttered Chaos might be interested. I emailed Laura… and, her response: "I was meaning to get in touch with you."

It took a while; Uttered Chaos had quite a backlog. But eventually the right time for *The Language of Stone* came around. Together Laura and I began digging into the various stone manuscripts I'd come up with over the years as a few new stone poems surfaced out of my brain. We polished and pruned, reorganized this way and that, and I like to think in the end we actually did come up with a jewel: this book you hold in your hand. Thank you to all who helped make *The Language of Stone* happen. Thank you for reading!

## ABOUT THE AUTHOR

Joan Dobbie wears several and varied hats. She's the mother of two grown children who have honored her with six grands. She spends many hours in airplanes chasing them all around the world. For twenty years she's been teaching Hatha Yoga at the University of Oregon and for about thirty years at Emerald Park. When she gets the chance, she makes clay sculptures. While wearing her writing hat, Joan focuses mostly on poetry, but an occasional short story or piece of creative nonfiction finds its way into her computer as well. Joan has a U of O MFA in Creative Writing. She co-hosts the monthly River Road Reading Series (RRRS). Her chapbooks include *A Trip through Mama Kali's Zoological Garden*, *Mother Earth Takes to Smoking*, *Quail Go Berzerk* and *Rocking My Father*. Full length books include *Before Us, Studies of Early Jewish families in Saint Lawrence County* (Temple Beth El), *The Many Faces of Hatha Yoga* (Kendall Hunt) and her "poemoir," *Woodstock Baby, A Novel in Poetry*. She writes Life Stories for elders who would like their histories recorded and will soon be conducting Poetry Immersion classes at Emerald Park in Eugene. Her poems and stories have appeared online and in mags and anthologies over the years. Some have won prizes.

riverroadreadings.blogspot.com | joandobbie.blogspot.com

# ACKNOWLEDGMENTS

Grateful acknowledgment is made to the editors of the following journals and presses for first publishing these poems or earlier versions of them:

In the poem "In Childhood," the phrase "trees of my childhood" is quoted from a poem by Lee Evans.

Goss, Erica. "Stone Poems," a video. Poems by Joan Dobbie "The Devil Decided," "How to have Sex with a Stone," "The Lost Stone," "Sometimes Stones Sing," and "Windowsill Gods." 2018.

Goss, Erica a video. "Stone Among Butterflies."

Riverwind, Asante created a CD that combines the music of Lotus Unfolding with readings of several of these poems.

## COLOPHON

Titles for *The Language of Stone* are set in Rockwell, a serif typeface modeled after Litho Antique™.

The body text itself is set in Garamond. It is a serif typeface, named for sixteenth-century Parisian engraver Claude Garamond.

www.ingramcontent.com/pod-product-compliance
Lightning Source LLC
LaVergne TN
LVHW041634070426
835507LV00008B/621